Presented to

_____

On the occasion of

_____

From

_____

Date

_____

ISBN 1-57748-561-0

Published by Barbour Publishing, Inc., P.O. Box 719, Uhrichsville, Ohio 44683
http://www.barbourbooks.com

 Member of the
Evangelical Christian
Publishers Association

Printed in China.

JUST FOR TODAY

Nancy Walker Hale

BARBOUR
PUBLISHING, INC.

INTRODUCTION

Some of us tend to live in the past, dwelling on our many failures, "what ifs," or the good old days. Others concentrate on the future, envisioning new projects and large-scale plans with only sleep interrupting their dreams of future successes. With brains churning on what might be, some are oblivious to the daily demands of consciously living each day to the fullest. But all of us who want to become more like Jesus must realize that our journey is a daily, continuous transformation, not a sudden onetime event that zaps us completely and forever into Christlike character. We must make conscious efforts, little by little, step by step, day by day, to see gradual progress and to gain insight into areas of our lives that need improvement. At times we are embarrassed and ashamed that we act selfishly, do not do any better than we do, and make the same mistakes over and over again. We declare this journey toward Christlikeness an impossible mission and want to bury our heads in the sand after every downfall. Evidently, the apostle Paul struggled with this same problem when he wrote to the early church, "I do not understand what I do. For what I want to do I do not do, but what I hate I do" (Romans 7:15 NIV). In spite of our shortcomings, we must be patient with ourselves and with others, as Christ is with us. ("Be kind and compassionate to one another, forgiving each other, just as in Christ God forgave you" Ephesians 4:32 NIV.)

My suggestions do not come from an elevated sense of my perfection—FAR FROM IT! I am merely acknowledging that the actions we take will make a difference in lives—the lives of others, and especially our own. It is easy to get discouraged when we try so hard to be Christlike and fail so many times in our lives. Why, then, should we continue to try to become more Christlike? In 2 Peter 1:3–4 we learn that God's divine power has given us everything we need for life and godliness. We may participate in His divine nature and escape the corruption in the world caused by evil desires. We need only to read a daily newspaper in practically any city to realize that our world needs people to model Christ's example. I, for one, want to leave this world a better place as a result of my being here and hope that my descendants and others will feel the same way. So, *Just For Today,* let us all take one step forward toward spreading God's love to others and allowing our thoughts and actions to be in line with His.

Just for Today...

I will let someone else get the credit for my work.

I will forget my troubles and put on a smile.

I will overlook a slight, intentional or not.

I will do something uplifting for someone less fortunate.

I will direct my thoughts toward others, not on myself.

I will listen more than I talk.

I will refrain from criticizing others.

I will take a break from the stresses of life.

I will let someone know how much I love them.

I will do something fun with a child.

I will give to a worthwhile charity.

I will get in touch with an old friend.

I will clean a messy area of my house.

Just for Today...

I will pamper myself.

I will plant a flower or a tree.

I will eliminate waste in one area of my life.

I will think before speaking.

I will end gossip when it reaches me.

I will take the first step in restoring a relationship.

I will clean up after myself.

I will refuse to pat myself on the back.

I will spend time with an elderly person.

I will compliment someone on a job well done.

I will enjoy sight.

I will push the plate away before second or third helpings.

Just for Today. . .

I will not be so straightlaced.

I will remember a veteran.

I will exercise my right to vote.

I will set an attainable goal.

I will reach a previously set goal.

I will celebrate life!

I will be kind to animals.

I will feed the ducks.

I will donate a few hours of my time to a worthwhile community activity.

I will change my routine.

I will eat healthy meals.

I will worship God.

Just for Today...

I will pay homage to an ancestor.

I will surprise someone pleasantly.

I will tell my parents how much
I appreciate their sacrifices for me.

I will relinquish a grudge.

I will congratulate someone else on her success.

I will exercise a part of my body other than my tongue.

I will greet others with a smile.

I won't worry about tomorrow.

I will change my "should have dones" to "dids."

I will give 110 percent to the task at hand.

I will visit a sick friend.

I will take time to listen to the birds sing.

Just for Today...

I will dismiss anger before it festers.

I will show gratitude for any act of kindness toward me.

I will force myself to be as mobile as possible.

I will not impose on friends.

I will plan a future event wisely.

I will pray for peace within my home.

I will be patient while waiting.

I will share something with another.

I will take the first step in conquering my fear.

I will not be a doormat for others.

I will give others enough personal space.

I will listen to another's opinion
without arguing or criticizing.

Just for Today. . .

I will pray for peace within my neighborhood.

I will pray for peace within my country.

I will pray for world peace.

I will keep myself morally straight.

I will read my Bible.

I will set a good example to others
who may be watching my actions.

I will be a person of integrity.

I will lead with authority.

I will begin to better myself.

I will block out unpleasant memories.

I will find something to laugh about.

I will scrub something until it sparkles.

Just for Today...

I will concentrate on purity.

I will show respect for another's belongings.

I will show appreciation to an authority figure.

I will be a mentor.

I will be thankful for the things I can do without pain.

I will support clean living by example.

I will set appropriate priorities regarding my time.

I will read something to broaden my knowledge.

I will get out into the fresh air instead of
staying cooped up inside.

I will leave a good tip for excellent service rendered.

I will put others before myself.

I will spend some time alone to
recharge my emotional batteries.

Just for Today...

I will spend time with God
to recharge my spiritual batteries.

I will recommit myself to a predetermined
but almost forgotten purpose.

I will save for something special instead of buying on credit.

I will be a friend in deed.

I will learn something new.

I will teach something helpful to someone.

I will forgive myself.

I will recycle.

I will be gentle.

I will count my blessings.

I will live in the present, not the past.

I will use caution.

Just for Today...

I will listen to good music.

I will relax.

I will put first things first.

I will reflect on how I might spend the rest of my life.

I will be less critical of others around me.

I will do a good deed for another
without expecting compensation.

I will be thankful for what I have.

I will become involved in something worthy of
my time and needy of my talents.

I will reminisce about the good times in my life,
rather than dwelling on the bad times.

I will spend more time in prayer for others
than for me and mine.

I will take action.

Just for Today...

I will eliminate a "want" in order to meet a "need."

I will be kind to all of God's creation.

I will direct my thoughts toward gratitude.

I will have my outlook be upward, not inward.

I will "be," not "do."

I will volunteer my money and time
for a greater cause than my desires.

I will be satisfied.

I will make the effort to smile whether I feel like it or not.

I will serve God.

I will be honest.

I will be hopeful concerning the future.

I will rejoice in the day that the Lord hath made.

I will endure my current circumstances.

Just for Today...

I will continue to work to reach a goal
in spite of opposition, ridicule, and interruptions.

I will seek to know God better.

I will try to be more Christlike in my actions and speech.

I will begin a new habit to improve my health.

I will be a cheerful giver.

*I will sing with my heart,
if not with my voice.*

I will give to "Caesar" what belongs to "Caesar."
(Pay taxes!)

I will give to God what belongs to God. (Tithe!)

I will complete a necessary task, no matter how unpleasant.

I will celebrate even the smallest victory
to encourage myself or others.

Just for Today. . .

I will be slow to become angry.

I will be fair.

I will persevere, if the going gets rough.

I will be determined to do what is right.

I will be an overcomer.

I will not hesitate when I see the opportunity to help another.

I will refrain from bragging.

I will show appreciation for a teacher.

I will be creative.

I will be an encourager.

I will be a friend.

I will be supportive.

I will be free from fears.

Just for Today...

I will be alert to perceive the needs of others.

I will be enthusiastic about life.

I will be a stimulating conversationalist.

I will be interesting and interested in
what others have to say.

I will be warm and friendly to those I meet.

I will keep a secret when asked to do so.

I will avoid procrastination.

I will avoid making mountains out of molehills.

I will have peace reign in my life.

I will have joy rule in my household.

I will do the work that is required of me and
not be concerned if others seem to have more by doing less.

I will be shrewd but innocent.

19

Just for Today. . .

I will not put myself in a prison of my own making
and limit what I should be doing.

I will heed a wiser person's advice.

I will value my freedoms.

I will rest and restore my soul.

I will improve my home in some way.

I will strengthen a relationship.

I will ponder God's perfect will for my life.

I will stifle my greed.

I will be a willing helper.

I will be a good neighbor,
regardless of what kind of neighbor I have.

I will brighten someone's day.

I will meet someone's need.

Just for Today...

I will not give up.

I will believe that help is just around the corner.

I will not yield to temptation to do wrong.

I will help someone going through a difficult time.

I will keep the end result in mind.

I will be quick to give sincere compliments.

I will refuse to make someone else miserable just because I am.

I will not harbor a grudge.

I will trust that my heartache will eventually turn to joy.

I will have confidence in myself.

I will treat others with respect
to maintain my own self-respect.

I will not nag.

I will not say, "I told you so."

Just for Today...

I will do something out of my comfort zone.

I will make my aches and pains invisible to others.

I will allow silence to be golden.

I will make clutter disappear from my desk.

I will not leave the gas tank on empty for the next driver.

I will challenge my mind.

I will not repeat yesterday's mistakes.

I will stretch my limits.

I will not allow garbage into my mind.

I will make music appreciation a part of my routine.

I will make recharging my "batteries" a priority.

I will plan an event to occur in the very near future,
to give me something to look forward to.

Just for Today...

I will send a note of appreciation to
someone who might least expect it.

I will have the courage to be the light that
exposes the darkness of wrongdoing.

I will be an exemplary role model for those around me.

I will not allow temporary frustrations and
disappointments to permanently alter my goals.

I will make Christ my role model.

I will let Christ's example, not peer expectations,
determine my decisions.

I will expand my horizons by doing something
totally foreign to my past experiences.

I will be the first to take the initiative
in standing up for righteousness.

Just for Today...

I will set up boundaries to protect me from destruction.

I will keep my head when all those around me do not.

I will have my desires be compatible with
God's desires for me.

I will make my emotional skin elephant-hide thick.

I will take a risk.

I will act as if I am courageous.

I will have faith that everything will turn out okay.

I will acquiesce to someone else's decision.

I will call someone who lives alone.

I will double-check my work to make sure
it was done correctly.

I will organize all the photographs
strewn around my house.

Just for Today. . .

I will do a task correctly, or not at all.

I will read a book that will challenge my thinking.

I will watch a "decent" movie uncluttered with violence, graphic sex scenes, or profanity.

*I will celebrate
someone's milestone birthday.
(Aren't they all?)*

I will praise a child for an accomplishment, big or small.

I will fill my mind with positive thoughts of the future, not negatives from the past.

I will do something that I enjoy doing along with the things I have to do.

I will take a carload of items to the Salvation Army or other charitable institution.

Just for Today. . .

I will keep moving although my body feels
as if it's full of lead.

I will donate a box of books to a library or school.

I will schedule that doctor's appointment
I've been putting off.

I will smile, anyway.

I will give a peace offering.

I will seek the good in people.

I will visit the nursing home and hug an older person.

I will clip a newspaper article about someone I know
and write a congratulatory note to mail with it.

I will clip a newspaper article of interest
to someone I know and mail it to them.

I will volunteer!

I will pray for the world economic situation.

Just for Today...

I will pray for the end of terrorism.

I will simplify my life by decreasing my debt.

I will update all my personal correspondence.

I will get rid of anything I haven't worn in two years.

I will apologize for acting out of character
during a moment of stress.

I will do the most important things first.

I will lean on God's strength, not my own.

I will pray for the country's politicians
during governmental chaos.

I will share the joy of answered prayer.

I will tell my child
(parent, spouse, friend, relative, neighbor, dog)
that I love them.

Just for Today . . .

I will refuse to force myself into a lane of traffic
that might place me or others in jeopardy.

I will escape from the whirlwind
of the daily grind with a cup of hot tea.

I will baby-sit for a young couple desperate for an evening
(or weekend) away from the draining demands of parenthood.

I will bake some cookies for a homebound person.

I will recycle magazines by giving them to a hospital,
nursing home, doctor's office, dentist's office, or hairdresser.

*I will realize that discipline must
accompany desire to achieve results.*

I will say grace in a restaurant.

I will send a "Thinking of You" card to
an acquaintance out of sight but not out of mind.

Just for Today. . .

I will join a widowed person on the church pew.

I will volunteer to help in the church nursery.

I will sing in the choir.

I will remember to record a momentous occasion
with a camcorder or camera.

I will be thrifty, but not stingy.

I will be a sermon in shoes—
I may be the only "Bible" some people read.

I will bring extra to a potluck supper.

I will contribute to the Scouts or any other
organizations training youth to be prepared
(not just for camp outs, but for life).

I will donate books currently collecting dust
to a worthwhile book sale.

Just for Today...

I will avoid impropriety.

I will be like a breath of fresh, rather than foul, air.

I will live a life pleasing to God.

I will keep an eye on quality, not quantity.

I will count my blessings instead of rehashing my burdens.

I will rest my weary bones before
they shout too loudly that I've waited too long.

I will hush evil thoughts as they attempt to enter my mind.

I will set my standards a little higher than before.

I will let someone go ahead of me in the checkout line,
especially if they have two items and I have twenty-two.

*I will ask God to give me
a job to do for Him, and then do it.*

I will do my best, no matter what I attempt to do.

Just for Today. . .

I will spend more time on my knees in prayer
than I did yesterday.

I will say no to a request that someone else should do
if I am already overextended.

I will refuse to fertilize my mind with the manure of malice.

I will enjoy life's spontaneity.

I will plant the seed of hope in someone
whose garden of life is currently full of weeds.

I will be an advocate to someone too weak
to speak for himself.

I will savor each moment of glory as if
it were a cup of water to parched lips.

I will mean what I say, and say what I mean.

I will disinfect myself of my own faults
before dissecting those of others.

31

Just for Today...

I will let discretion be my ally.

I will not allow the warped values of the world
to invade my personal convictions.

I will choose to be joyful.

I will recognize unwanted interruptions as
opportunities for ministry rather than reasons for frustration.

I will use my minutes wisely since they
disappear as rapidly as snowflakes melt.

I will chase away unwholesome thoughts.

I will make injustice my adversary.

I will accept my past.

I will make humor a part of my routine.

I will live God's Way.

I will spread good news, not the opposite.

Just for Today...

I will give some time that I can't really spare
to lend a listening ear to a needy soul.

I will ask a children's home what it needs, and provide it,
even if it is just a pack of pencils.

I will offer to relieve someone who is
sitting with a bedfast family member.

I will pretend that my problems don't exist.

I will deny the urge to burst someone's bubble.

I will overcome timidity and speak up for righteousness.

I will nip a budding sin before it blooms
into a prickly cactus.

I will let Jesus collect five minutes' worth of my tears
and 23 hours and 55 minutes of my praise.

I will refuse to accept for myself
any honor belonging to God.

Just for Today. . .

I will leave vengeance in the Lord's hands.

I will leave my heavy bag of false guilt with Jesus.

I will muzzle my mouth when
volcanic acid threatens to spew.

I will meditate on past deliverance from troubles.

I will practice mercy.

I will forget past slights against me.

I will do a good deed in secret.

I will carry someone else's burden.

I will guard the door of my heart from Satan's attacks.

I will shield my mind from coveting other's
wealth, status, or beauty.

I will be pleasant to live with.

I will listen to my own heart's desires.

I will spend the day as though it were my last.

I will not let others intimidate me.

I will have moderation as my motto.

I will make compassion my creed.

I will memorize Scripture.

I will clear my thoughts of any plots to "get even."

I will be a better money manager.

I will be a proper steward of all that
God has entrusted to me.

I will increase my vitality by decreasing my stress.

I will make a list and complete three of
the most important things on it.

I will begin to build a support system to
help me through the valleys of my life.

I will deplete the envy reservoir in my life.

I will maintain the proper balance in my life.

I will return a borrowed item—with interest.

I will awaken with a thankful heart.

I will give my undivided attention
when someone speaks to me.

I will wash my hands of anything reeking of deceit.

I will believe that God will give me the desires of my heart.

I will put my troubles and work aside and read a good book.

I will harbor fresh goodwill toward others
instead of aging grudges.

I will muster enough resources to be energetic.

I will strive to reach the potential that
God had in mind when He created me.

Just for Today...

I will hate unholiness.

I will perform at an optimum level
in whatever I do.

I will consider tomorrow in view of
the consequences of today's moments.

I will toss away unhealthy coping methods in my life.

I will reinforce good behavior (in myself and in others).

I will back up my convictions with appropriate actions.

I will wear a pleasant look on my face.

I will listen to quality music.

I will make a list of things for which I am thankful.

I will erase the memory of,
but not the lessons from, past errors.

I will obey God's laws.

I will stitch up small tears in relationships before
they become major ones.

I will do it right the first time.

I will be a friend to the friendless.

I will concentrate on the pluses, not the minuses.

I will not let discouragement creep in like
a heavy fog obscuring my vision.

I will open my home to others with warm hospitality.

I will shelter an abused person,
if not physically, then with prayer.

I will shut the door on the disgusting habits
that try to enter my life.

I will have contentment walk beside me.

I will stamp out the irritating bugs within my personality.

Just for Today...

I will allow humility to shield me from
the hailstones of superiority.

I will have Christ-confidence that will bolster me from
the invasion of inferiority.

I will turn my best intention into an even better deed.

I will brush any chips off my shoulder before
they fall and mash my (or someone else's) toes.

I will yield to the temptation of doing
an anonymous good deed.

I will cover my day with prayer.

I will expect the best to happen, not imagine the worst.

I will adapt my behavior to suit each circumstance.

I will acquaint myself with all of my closest neighbors.

I will snub no one.

Just for Today. . .

I will tread gently on other's fragile emotions.

I will confess my sins of commission.

I will confess my sins of omission.

I will dissolve misunderstandings.

I will create a happy moment for myself or for others.

I will persevere,
persevere, persevere.

I will face the person in the mirror with enthusiasm!